I Think (

Simone Braxton

SOCiAL AND EMOTiONAL LEARNiNG
FOR THE REAL WORLD™

Rosen Classroom™

So much can happen in one day!

It's good to look at what I did.

I find a quiet place.
I sit and think.

What did I do to help others?

What did I do that hurt others?

What can I do tomorrow?

Words to Know

help

hurt

think